The Art of Grooming:

A Philosophical Approach to Dog Grooming

By: Jun S. Yun

Edited by: Tiffany Moses

Special Thanks:

Ted Woehrle: Thank you so much for sharing your wisdom and experience with me. This book would never have been accomplished without your encouragement and your help. Thank you for all your time and your belief in me.

Tiffany Moses: I truly appreciate all the effort you put into helping me with publishing this book. Thank you for sharing my vision for the future of dog grooming.

Pam Lauritzen: Thank you for all you have done for the grooming industry, and for groomers all around the world. Your passion and courage inspires me, and this book is a testament to the impact you made on my life.

Cesar Milan: Thank you so much for your life. Namaste, my brother, and thank you for the inspiration you have given to millions around the world. Practicing Cesar's Way has totally changed my life, and my grooming philosophy would not be complete without it.

Table of Contents:

Preface:

The Art of Grooming: My Philosophical View on Dog Grooming

In my opinion, dog grooming is the ultimate dog experience. The inspiration for the title to this book came to me while I was reading The Art of Happiness: A Handbook for Living by His Holiness the Dalai Lama, and Howard C. Cutler. I realized while reading the book that it was a philosophy on happiness, and not so much a guide to happiness. It was a way to view happiness, which is what we are all ultimately striving to achieve in our lives. We all want to have and experience genuine happiness. However the Dalai Lama tells us "There is no way to happiness, happiness is the way." I also realized that Sun Tzu's The Art of War doesn't teach us how to wield a sword and shield just like the Art of Happiness doesn't teach us how to smile and laugh in all situations. I wanted to write a book that would describe a way to be calm and confident while grooming any dog under any circumstances. Rather than teach how to use the shears and clippers properly, or how to set the perfect pattern, this book is intended to provide a unique perspective on dog grooming. My hope for everyone who reads this book to achieve a beautiful experience no matter what the circumstances are. When we change the way we feel about grooming, the experience changes for both the groomer and the dog.

I have always had a deep connection with dogs ever since I was a child. There was never a time a dog was not by my side. I remember as a child my best friend was my neighbor's dog, Bear. Bear was a beautiful Samoyed, and we used to walk together around the trails near our house all day. There were times when I would crawl into the doghouse with a dog or sleep with my roommate's dog during my college years. I would talk to them for hours, but they would do most of the talking – I'm a good listener. In the 3rd grade, at a Christian private school, I drew a St. Bernard with a Bible attached to his collar. The St. Bernard is a noble dog bred to help people who were stranded in the snowy mountains. They would carry food and drink around their necks and find people who were buried or hidden in snow with their incredible sense of smell. These dogs were specifically bred to save human lives. I convinced the principle of the school to change the school mascot from an Eagle to this St. Bernard with a Bible that I drew. Dogs are, in my opinion, the most noble of God's creations and they have always made me feel happy. They do anything to please us, and they do so in a manner that tells us that it is their highest privilege to do so. By taking the time and spending the energy to comb and brush them, we are telling them how much we love them. Love is action. We do it because we love them, and they love us back for it. Love takes action.

All my life dogs have given me a way to get through the toughest times – both emotionally and physically.

Without my dogs I would not have walked while I suffered from intense back pain due to two ruptured, herniated discs. Because of dog grooming I not only have a way to provide a good life for my family, but I've also become a better person because of it. A lot of the information in this book came to me when I wasn't even looking for it. I couldn't have actively sought this information out because I didn't even know what I didn't know. When I first sat in Pam Lauritzen's Best of the Masters grooming seminars, I was only there to get a certificate at the end of the series. I wasn't there to learn anything. I was foolish and arrogant enough to think that I already knew everything. From the moment I sat down and saw a picture of a dog's pore to the moment she wrapped up, I was completely floored. At the end of the lecture I went up to thank her for what she was doing, and the information she shared with me profoundly changed the course of my grooming career and my personal life.

Anyone who is interested in grooming a dog – whether it's your own dog or someone else's – can benefit from reading this book with an open mind. I truly hope this book enriches your grooming experiences and enhances the relationships you have with your dogs. As dog groomers we share a passion and a love for dogs that few people are able to understand because you can only gain an understanding of it by doing it. Like riding a bike. Once you learn how to ride a bike, it is a skill you have forever. My hope is that by reading this book grooming becomes a beautiful and intimate experience for you that promotes inner peace, healing and happiness for both you and the dogs you groom. Rather than focus on the techniques and tools, I focus on the principles and intentions. Even though we groom dogs to help them, if it is against their will or if we cause them unintentional damage, we must be willing to reconsider our actions. This book is intended to provide a new perspective on dog grooming, and explain how that can help us maintain a calm, positive experience. "When you change the way you look at things, the things you look at change" Wayne Dyer. This is the Art of Grooming. Thank you so much for reading.

Chapter 1: The Importance of Grooming

To understand the importance of grooming, we should first define what proper dog grooming is. We do not have to agree on one definition, but in order to provide consistency throughout this book I would like to offer my opinion of what proper dog grooming is. Grooming a dog properly, to me, is much like grooming myself properly. I don't visit my hairstylist everyday or even every month, but I do take care of my hair daily. Proper grooming is proper hygiene. We don't visit the dentist everyday, but we do brush our teeth several times a day – ideally. When we are checking our dog's teeth and gums, when we clean their ears, when we clip their nails or brush their coats we are grooming them. I could sum up my entire philosophy on dog grooming in one sentence: Brush more, and bathe less. When people think of dog grooming most of the time they think about washing and trimming the dog. The bath and haircut is definitely a part of dog grooming, but they are only parts of grooming just like showering and getting our haircut would be the parts of what it takes to keep ourselves properly groomed. It would be like saying that love is sex. Sex is definitely a part of love, but to say that two people are only in love if they have sex with one another would be ridiculous! The reason I use sex as an example is because grooming a dog – just like making love with a partner – is a very intimate experience and it requires mutual trust and respect. It cannot be forced or rushed. When two people engage in a physical act of love it is beautiful, and we call that making love. When it is unwanted by either one, the same act becomes something unspeakable. This is the way we should view grooming – the same experience can provide comfort and healing, or anxiety and pain. We do not have to hit a dog to traumatize them. A dog can be traumatized emotionally by ignoring their body language and what they are telling us. If we are to be around their most sensitive areas, we must first take the time to gain their permission.

For ease of reading, I will refer to proper dog grooming simply as "grooming." The average dog owner usually isn't aware that they have very unrealistic expectations of the bath. It would be unreasonable to think that the water from our showerhead would wash off our dirty underwear. We have to physically remove our clothes before washing ourselves because the soap and water can only do so much. Otherwise it would probably be better not to wash at all. No matter how well I tried to hide it, if I continued to wash in the same underwear and undershirt without ever taking them off, the effects would eventually show. This is what is happening to our dogs. They have millions of dead hair still stuck in the pores along with oils, bacteria, mites, and other cellular debris that we are expecting the specially formulated shampoo and water to just wash away. Eventually the accumulated effects of cellular damage to the skin takes its toll on our old friends and it begins to show when they are around 4 or 5 years old, but sometimes even sooner than that. The effects that finally show up are lumps, bumps, and greasy, flakey skin. Some people refer to them as "skin tags" or "old dog bumps", but they are actually skin eruptions. Pores get so clogged and backed up that it actually erupts out of the skin and looks like a tiny raisin hanging off of the skin. Another reaction is it turns into a mass under the skin that eventually turns into an uncomfortable lump or even a tumor. Although it takes several years for this to happen, and it takes time to help the skin return back to balance, it is never too late to begin providing your dog with proper hygiene.

So how do we remove the dog's dirty "underwear"? We do this by removing the dead hairs that are inside the skin. This is what is called "carding" in the grooming industry. Carding simply means to pull out dead hairs, and a carding tool is any tool used to achieve that goal. The dead hairs are easy to spot because they're lifeless and they don't lie nicely like the live hairs. They're soft, fuzzy, discolored and will look frayed. These hairs must be removed prior to the bath. We must comb and brush most of it out so that the water and shampoo can clean and condition the pores. The bath is really for the skin not the coat because only a healthy skin can produce a healthy coat. The water can only do so much. Just like it doesn't wash off our dirty clothes, it will not wash away the dead, transitioning hairs that are still inside the pores. It is better not to wash your dog if you cannot give him a thorough combing and brushing before washing him. I do not expect people to suddenly brush and comb their dogs daily, I certainly don't, but I am asking that they do a good job of it before the bath. Just like a horse should be brushed daily and washed occasionally when it becomes necessary, we should brush more and bathe our dogs less. However, since horses don't sleep with us or sit on our furniture I understand the need to wash our dogs more than our horses. I am simply asking that we take the time to remove the dead coat before we begin washing them. Carding the dog after the bath is still acceptable, but that would be like taking off our underwear after we get out of the shower. It would work better than keeping them on and drying them, but it is still preferable to remove them before the shower.

The haircut and style is what most groomers and dog owners are focused on so I believe it is important for the dog to look good. However, it is my personal belief that it is much more important to feel good than it is to look good. I want the dog to feel his best so he'll look his best. A happy dog is a beautiful dog! Grooming to me is a lifestyle, not a job. It is a labor of love like we engage in for all of our family members. It's checking their teeth and ears, combing and brushing them regularly to help them feel comfortable. If you ever watch dogs in a pack relaxing, there are usually a couple that are licking each other in areas like their ears and nibbling at each other. What they are doing is showing affection and strengthening the bond by grooming each other. In your dog's mind, when you brush him you are solidifying your bond with him. Brushing also helps evenly distribute the natural oils all throughout their coat to give it a natural shine that protects them from dust and water. So much must happen before a dog can be washed and trimmed. Just like painting a wall properly involves much more than selecting and putting up a new color, steps must be taken in order to give the dog a bath. It takes a lot of time and energy, I understand, but this is the most important part of grooming a dog. An improper groom can never stand the test of time, and just like paint on a wall, it will eventually show.

The impact that grooming has on a dog's life is huge. The important thing to keep in mind is that we seldom ever see the positive or negative impact the groom had on the dog until later on down the road. The canine skin and coat is a living system. It is like a rainforest with its own natural flora. When we go in there and interfere or disrupt the natural environment, we should know what we are doing and how it will affect the skin. Dogs, like horses, should not be washed too often because it damages their skin. When we add chemicals and ingredients we know nothing about onto their skin, we are gambling with our dog's health and comfort. I believe that as groomers we have a big responsibility to learn what is in our products and research them before we make a decision to use them on our dogs. Then it will be an informed decision and our dogs will appreciate that immensely. Everything we do during the groom should all be done with the end goal in mind. Everything we do should be with the purpose of helping the dog look and feel their best.

The haircut is like selecting the best outfit that will highlight each individual dog's best features while hiding any flaws. Just like our clothes should highlight our best attributes and help us look attractive to others, the haircut should accentuate the dog's strong points. When deciding on the style of the trim, I always take a step back and look at the dog for a moment to study it. We want the eyes to be drawn to the center and all the lines should look like they all flow smoothly connecting one area of the dog to another in perfect balance. If the haircut is done properly, it will last for several weeks and will hold its shape as it grows out. The haircut is only a small part of grooming that is only done every 6-8 weeks, which is why many of us say that we should only groom our dogs once every couple of months. Now that we have a better understanding of what grooming is and why it is so important, we can understand that grooming should actually be done daily. My wife and I have a pediatrician, a dentist, and a hairstylist for our daughters; however, maintaining proper hygiene for my girls is our responsibility on a daily basis. I will admit that I do not brush my own dogs on a daily basis because after a long day of grooming I am not exactly thrilled about the idea. However, I will make time during the weekend and I use that time to think while I brush out their coat. By doing this you will be helping your dogs feel more comfortable and look much better, and the rewards they will bring you in return are immeasurable.

Chapter 2: The Importance of Breathing and Visualization

Grooming, in my opinion is the ultimate dog experience. No other activity requires that amount of time, trust and cooperation. We are in their most intimate spaces: poking, prodding, clipping, etc. Not even a vet spends that much time while asking for that much cooperation. It has taught me to control myself when I feel anxious, worried, upset or frustrated. This has helped me tremendously with how I view problems and difficulties. By becoming a better groomer I've become a better husband, father and friend. I've become a better person and I now know what it feels like to love my life. I owe all of this to the noble dogs that I have been honored to work with. It is because of this intense feeling of gratitude that I have towards my canine friends that I have decided to write this book. I owe it to them.

The grooming experience is one of the most intimate moments we are blessed to share with our dogs. Every groom can be a beautiful experience – one that is healing for both the dog and the groomer. It all depends on our approach. How you approach any situation is important, but it is vital when it comes to grooming a dog. If you are nervous or anxious about it, you're more than likely to have an unpleasant experience. I used to struggle with every dog I groomed, particularly with the nails. I used to be nervous about clipping nails because I was scared of accidentally making the nail bleed. It always seems to be stressful for both the dog and myself. It's hard to accept, but the problem began before I ever approached the dog. I've made quite a reputation for myself here in Atlanta as the guy everyone calls when they have a "problem" dog – whether it's an aggressive, nervous, or hyper dog it doesn't matter to me. The problem is never the dog, but my response to the dog and how I approach him. I now know that I can successfully groom any dog no matter how difficult they have been in the past. However, this was not always the case.

Being calm and confident does not come naturally to me. Before I got into grooming dogs I used to worry a lot, and I would often fear the worst. I would toss and turn at nights and I was always full of anxiety, and nervous about everything. Working with dogs has helped me to control my thoughts and emotions – to live in the moment. By having to work with them so closely it taught me a lot about myself. I realized that I had so many flaws in my character that I've ignored or denied all my life. It showed me how much work I had to do on my personal character. A wise man once told me, "Personality may open doors, but its character that keeps them open." When I started working as a dog bather I was overweight, taking pain medications for my chronic back pain, smoked cigarettes regularly, and would often get irritable with people I care about. I am now pain-free, happy and free of any medications along with the dangerous addiction to cigarettes. I am a completely changed man all thanks to becoming a dog groomer. If we are open to it, dogs can teach you to be a better human being by helping us develop our characters. Once the strategies in this book are practiced, you will experience self-confidence and feel empowered in a way that will have positive effects on every area of your life – not just dog grooming.

Anyone who has ever played a sport, an instrument or had to perform in front of a large audience understands the importance of visualization. A very good friend of mine who played soccer most of her life told me that her coaches would always emphasize the importance of positive visualization. Positive visualization is simply imagining a situation happening exactly the way you want it to happen before it actually happens. See yourself doing something perfectly before you approach it. Our minds are powerful! Henry Ford once said, "Whether you think you can or think you can't, you're right." We must have faith in ourselves and believe that we have the ability to help our dogs look and feel their best.

In order to become an extraordinary groomer, you must have an extraordinary imagination. A clear picture of the end result you desire is the blueprint to a well-groomed dog. Before actually grooming the dog, first see the entire session going well. See yourself washing a calm and cooperative dog that is grateful for your efforts. See the dog offering you his nails for trimming because he totally trusts you. See it all going so well. It is such an incredibly intimate experience that is literally a labor of love, and your dog appreciates you doing for him that which he cannot do for himself. Now ask yourself, "Do I believe this is going to happen?" Until the answer is an honest "yes", you cannot hope for it to really happen. If the answer is "no", it's totally fine – that's ok. The key is to be honest with yourself and saying "yes" does no good if you don't really believe it. "No" simply means that you are now aware of what you want and that your belief in attaining it must change. Anthony Hopkins delivered many great lines in his movies, but my favorite line is in the movie the Edge where he shouts, "Whatever one man can do another man can do!" The best way to believe in yourself and change the way you think is to change the way you feel by breathing and relaxation techniques.

Breathing is something that is so obviously important that we often overlook just how important it really is. Ask any professional singer or athlete how important it is to breathe properly and they will talk your ear off. The technique is called diaphragmatic breathing, but to put it simply it is breathing deeply with your belly rather than your chest. Just by focusing on our breathing we become more aware of the moment and everything in it. I have two herniated discs, bad knees and flat feet. It used to hurt after a long day of grooming; sometimes to the point I would worry about having to quit due to the pain. I am now pain-free and enjoy the long days of grooming. I even have energy at the end of the day to do the things I like to do, like cook a delicious dinner for my family. My body felt much better when I began practicing diaphragmatic breathing. I now catch myself several times throughout the groom holding my breath during tense moments or when making precision cuts. When I am aware of my breathing I am immediately aware of muscles that are tensed and my body posture. Then I realize that I'm not in a comfortable position and I readjust to a position that is more relaxed and controlled. By breathing correctly we become more aware of the moment and we become more centered. Our heart rate slows, our bodies relax and our minds become sharper.

It is not by physical force but a calm and centered mind that a relationship is formed with the dog. Like any relationship that is worth having, you cannot force it or try to rush it. It must happen naturally and feel effortless. Everything that happens first happens in the mind. Breathe deeply through your belly and close your eyes. Visualize the grooming session again and feel yourself believing you can do it with every breath you take. Once you feel calm and confident believing that you have everything within you to accomplish anything you set your mind to, you are ready to begin grooming. I began this chapter with the example of clipping nails because this is the area most people, even professional groomers like myself, have trouble with. My wife is the sweetest and most caring person you will ever meet, but she used to have such difficulty keeping it together when she would clip nails. I would see her face turn red when the dog would continue to fight or protest. Then she started practicing breathing techniques like slowly and deeply breathing through her belly until she was calm. She would visualize the dog relaxing and accepting the activity while inhaling, and then clip a nail during the exhales. She is now a nail clipping master if there is such a thing.

Rather than focus on techniques and strategies, try to be more aware of the moment and be creative when it comes to the challenging parts of the groom. Because every dog is different the approach and specific plan of action will also have to be different with every dog, but these two factors of the approach will always be the same for every dog we groom. Believe the groom will go well while visualizing it happening, and remember to breathe. Also make sure to put cell phones and watches away. Not because they may get wet, but because they are distractions. This is our time to bond with our dog, to connect with her the way nature intended. Forget time exists. Clear your schedule for the day and don't take any calls or reply to any messages. All of that can wait. Right now we are earning the trust, respect and love our dog has for us by giving her the gift of our time and attention. The rewards we will reap in return are immeasurable. They will not understand that we must be at a meeting in two hours. All they know is that we are feeling tense so they will tense up too causing us to feel frustrated or upset that this is not happening fast enough. They will not understand that we're only feeling this way because we have other responsibilities to tend to. They will think that we are frustrated or upset with them. This is what causes the unpleasant experiences. When we are tense and rushing can we blame the dog for not liking bath time? So just breathe, relax, and enjoy yourself. This is the ultimate dog experience – there is no need to rush it.

Chapter 3: The Importance of Body Language: Energy

By learning to communicate with our thoughts and our body language, we are showing our dogs that we are trying to speak to them in their own language. If one of my mother's clients suddenly tried to speak to her in Korean, she would be impressed regardless of proper grammar or pronunciation. Just the fact that they were trying would touch her. That is the way our dogs feel when we stop speaking to them and start communicating with them. Whether we know it or not we are constantly communicating with our dogs. They are masters at reading our body language and picking up our energy. Einstein said, "Everything is energy." Everything we see is actually a collection and combination of molecules vibrating in a certain way to make up what we see. We are all made up of molecules that are made up of atoms. When we begin to go into the subatomic level and zoom in to the very furthest possible level, there is nothing. This "nothing" is something, and the Chinese call it "Chi". Many cultures in Asia are very familiar with the concept of Chi – the life force that is in every living thing. Bob Proctor said, "Whether you look through the lens of a microscope or a telescope the view is equally breathtaking." When we understand that our thoughts are connected to our emotions that give off energy that radiates through our bodies, it helps us to become more aware of our thoughts and feelings. "If you are ever unsure how you are feeling, just look at your dogs. They mirror your energy." Cesar Milan

By communicating our intentions effectively we will create a calm environment for the dog to relax in. This will eliminate the majority of accidental injuries that can happen during a groom. From the moment a dog sees us she is reading our energy – our body language, and the scent we carry. The best way to get her comfortable with us and trust us is to be calm and centered. Do not baby talk or get all excited – this is not the time for that. I've seen many groomers and owners go into an excited, high-pitch baby talk mode and overwhelm the dog. They need to know that this is not playtime – that comes after the groom as a reward. Every activity has its proper time and place – we wouldn't expect the nurse taking our blood pressure to scream "UNO!" into our ear because it would not be the right time for that. She needs us to stay calm and still so she can help us. In order to be calm while we groom dogs they must trust us, and a bond must be formed. We should always stay in the moment and focused on what we are doing. Most accidents happen when we look away for a moment – just a moment. Even if someone tries to talk to us, we should not turn our attention away from the dog. It may seem rude to them, but just explain that you are totally zoned in with your dog at the moment and you cannot sever the bond. They will most likely think you have temporarily lost your mind and will leave you alone for the time being.

The best way to establish a bond and create a relationship is by walking together. "Fish swim, birds fly, dogs walk" Cesar Milan. Dogs have to walk together as a pack in order to form strong bonds. To them it is like having a long conversation. Like any friendship, the more shared experiences and activities you have together the stronger the bond becomes. When walking with the dog I recommend practicing Cesar's Way: Calm, assertive energy. Walk confidently and do not let the dog pull or dart in every direction. We want them by our side or slightly behind us in order to keep them focused on the activity of walking. This sets the stage for a smooth grooming session. This will put us in a "leadership" role in the dog's mind because we are leading him during the walk. We want him to relieve himself during the walk, but let it be on our terms not his. In accomplishing an effective walk we gain his trust and respect while also making sure he is comfortable during the grooming session. Many times dogs are uncooperative simply because they have to go potty. While walking, practice the visualization and breathing techniques described in the previous chapter. This is the perfect time for it. It will help you get in tune with nature and form a connection – a bond – with the dog you are about to groom. Think of the movie Avatar when he rides the horse or flies the dragons. He connects with them with his hair so that they can get in tune with each other. When we take the time to form the bond, we earn the right to groom them. This is a respectful way for us to ask permission from them.

While enjoying our walk, we should try to be silent and aware of the moment. Try not to speak to him while walking together. Just enjoy the bonding experience and be aware of every moment. Visualize and think positive thoughts as if he can read your mind. This is truer than you would think. When I need a dog to stand still or stand up from a sitting position, I usually ask by gently touching and projecting a thought – I ask with my mind. I call it Jedi Grooming. For those of you who are not familiar with Star Wars, a Jedi is a sci-fi version of a Shaolin Monk. Instead of Chi, in Star Wars it is called the Force. There is a dark side to the Force and those who practice it are called Siths. Dog groomers who are nervous, anxious, fearful, worried or have any negative thoughts or emotions must make a conscious effort to become more calm and relaxed. Confident and firm when necessary, but never forceful, or they run the risk of becoming a Sith Groomer. If you watch Star Wars one thing you will notice about Jedi's is that they are peaceful and rely on the power of their minds rather than physical strength. They use the force to help and protect, and if they do use it against their enemies it is only to push them. Siths use the force to control and dominate. They physically harm people by electrocuting them or choking them. Jedi Groomers use the power of their minds and calm, assertive energy to make suggestions that are helping the dog. Sith Groomers yell and use physical force to control and restrain a dog. They cause harm to the dogs while grooming them because they cannot control their own thoughts and emotions. "Be mindful of your thoughts," the Jedi would say. I like to think of myself as a Jedi when it comes to grooming because I rely on the power of intention and positive visualization.

Our bodies emit an electromagnetic field around us that can actually be measured by scientists using medical devices that are available today. I was listening to Jack Canfield, the author of Chicken Soup for the Soul, and he was saying that our thoughts produce electrical frequencies that can be measured outside of our bodies. Our emotions produce an even stronger electromagnetic pulse that resonates throughout our bodies and even change our physical state. When we feel anger our heart rate and blood pressure go up. When we feel gratitude and love our bodies begin healing itself and we emit positive energy all around us. Always be in this state of gratitude and love, which will help you to be calm and assertive as Cesar Milan teaches. Once you have mastered your own thoughts and emotions your grooming sessions will always be a pleasant experience for both you and your dog.

In an article in the Groomer to Groomer Magazine, published by Barkleigh Productions Inc. in the October issue of 2013, titled "Golden Heroes" by Kathy Salzberg there is mention of this electromagnetic field. The article was written about an army veteran named David R. Cantara who rescues and trains Golden Retrievers to help war veterans who suffer from Post Traumatic Stress

Disorder (PTSD). "Golden Retrievers are David's breed of choice for this work because of their calm nature, trainability, and physical strength... In addition, these dogs have been proven to be highly susceptible to the bio waves or vibrations that emanate from a person, picking up on anxiety buildup and thus forewarning a panic attack... As these dogs support their owners, they do everything from alleviating anxiety with a gentle nudge to interrupting nightmares, turning on lights, and searching the house for intruders." Dogs have such a way of connecting with us that they can pick up on our "bio waves". We cannot underestimate the connection an owner has with their dog. I've heard before that groomers can be rough with dogs if we need to be because the owner will never know. I disagree. I believe that the owners are just too nice or uncomfortable to say anything, but they know when something's not right. When we treat them with love and respect, they will respond to us in kind.

Many times we feel anxiety or frustration as a result of challenging circumstances or a very unruly dog. We must choose to be calm and remember that we do not have to fall prey to our doubts and fears. We are artists. We have greatness inside of us. I often wonder how differently horses would act towards their predators if they realized how massive and powerful they really are. I was having this conversation with a taxi driver one night, and he pointed out to me that they can't think that way because they are prey animals. There was a silence for a moment before I asked him, "What if we have unlimited potential inside of us, but we live in fear like prey animals do simply because we can't think differently? What if all we have to do is change our minds and see ourselves differently in order to live fearlessly?" We are not horses – we are not prey. As dog groomers we are fearless and courageous. We do what many others do not do in spite of any pain or fear/anxiety we may have. We do it because we love them, and that love cannot be physically expressed without us. Keep these intentions and thoughts in your mind, and they will be projected out as energy that the dog will be able to understand through your body language.

Chapter 4: The Language of Touch: Touch Therapy and Pressure Points

One of the best sermons I remember hearing as a child was on the healing power of a loving touch. It was about an orphanage where the baby closest to the door would always do far better than the other babies that were in the room in every area of development. They were happier and healthier than the rest and the director of the orphanage wanted to know why it was always the baby closest to the door? It turned out that every night the lady caretaker would hold the baby closest to the door and gently rock them and talk to them before leaving the room. It was only a few minutes each night but that was enough to make a world of difference for that one child that received the loving touch of a caring hand. Touch is powerful and so essential for wellbeing.

I found a study that has been done more recently in Korea. "A group of Korean infants under the care of an orphanage were provided with an extra 15 minutes of stimulation twice a day, 5 times a week, for 4 weeks. The additional stimulation consisted of auditory (female voice), tactile (massage), and visual (eye-to-eye contact). Compared to the infants who only received regular care, the stimulated orphans gained significantly more weight and had larger increases in body length and head circumference after the 4 week intervention period, as well as at 6 months of age. In addition, the stimulated infants had fewer illnesses and clinic visits." Kim, T., Shin,

Y., & White-Traut, R. (2003). Multisensory Intervention Improves Physical Growth and Illness Rates in Korean Orphaned Newborn Infants. Research in Nursing and Health, 26(6):424-33. The power of a loving touch has a lasting, healing effect.

Understanding the power of touch will give you the ability to groom with total confidence and ease. It is not about touching our dogs, biting each other is considered touching, but knowing how to touch our dogs. The way we touch them, and the intentions behind the touch have everything to do with how the dog reacts to you. When grooming a hyper or nervous dog sometimes you will notice yourself holding your breath. Once you are aware of that you'll also notice that your body is tense and your grip on the dog may be much more firm then necessary. As soon as you recognize what is going on than the solution is immediate and happens naturally. Take a deep breath through your belly, not your chest, and feel yourself becoming calm. Now imagine you are a nurse taking blood from child. Touch and hold with the intention only to help and a feeling. Remember that your grip and your actions all communicate your intentions of helping. We all know that "Love is patient, love is kind..." Right now you are a dog groomer, you are love in action, which means you are patient and you are kind.

We must adopt these ideas and be willing to try to put them into practice by exercising the power of our minds. Having merely an intellectual knowledge of these concepts will do us no good. We must integrate them into our grooming sessions and experience the feeling for ourselves. It is one thing to read about making a garden, it is quite another to actually do it. I had the unique experience in my childhood to build an enormous garden with my grandfather before he passed away. Looking back it was one of the best experiences of my life, but while I was going through it there were several occasions that I thought I was going to die. I had never encountered such a physically and mentally challenging experience until then and it hurt. However, I learned that you cannot just download a farm from the Internet. Nature requires time and effort, and that is what we must keep in mind when trying to build a relationship with the dogs we groom. My wife has heard my philosophical rants about dog grooming, and how we should all aspire to become Jedi's ever since we met. But even she was astonished at times. It is not anything about me physically, but rather my approach and the way I touch that makes the difference. Each of us possesses all that is necessary to accomplish an extraordinary groom – but we must believe in ourselves. When we touch a fearful dog fearfully, we cannot achieve balance. We must touch them calmly and with total confidence.

How we touch – the intentions behind the touch – has everything to do with the reaction we get from the dog we are grooming. They need to feel calm, healing energy that comes through the practice and use of proper breathing and visualization techniques that we covered in the previous chapters. Now that we have an understanding on how to touch, I would like to briefly discuss where to touch. There are certain areas on a dog that you can touch in order to help alleviate pain or discomfort. The energy that we covered in Chapter 2, called Chi, flows all throughout the dog's body traveling along pathways called meridians, which are energy lines. These energy lines have points where they intersect called pressure points. According to TCM (Traditional Chinese Medicine) concepts, all illnesses and negative/unwanted behaviors can be traced to a deficiency in the flow of Chi to a certain area. They believe that by balancing the flow of Chi through touch therapy we can help restore the body to its natural state of wellbeing.

"Acupressure connects you and your dog with thousands of year of natural healing. It's a gentle yet powerful healing tool based on Traditional Chinese Medicine (TCM). Our dogs need not know the theories and concepts that underlie acupressure and TCM. They will thoroughly appreciate the feeling of health and well-being leaving the understanding and richness of knowledge to you." Snow, Amy; Zidonis, Nancy, "Acu-Dog: A Guide to Canine Acupressure" pg. 5

Acupressure is a way to communicate our intentions to help the dog in a way the dog immediately understands. Because groomers do not usually have the luxury of time, we must have a way to gain the dog's trust rather quickly so that the grooming session does not run all day long. I can talk the dog's ear off in the tub and tell him my entire life story leading up to becoming a groomer – he wouldn't care one bit. However, if I touch him in a way that promotes relaxation and calmness, he immediately understands who I am by my touch. When I groom a dog I always try to incorporate many, if not all, acupressure points and gently massage them as I lather the shampoo, and when I massage the conditioner into the coat. Sometimes there are situations and circumstances that prevent being able to, but it is always good to have an understanding of pressure points and knowing which ones can benefit the dog you are grooming. Remember to always touch with the intention of love and a willingness to help them. I sing love songs and inspirational songs to them, which seems to help tremendously with nervous/fearful dogs. This is love in action, a labor of love, and the benefits for your relationship with your dog will be indescribable. We must show them that we are humans worthy of their trust and cooperation. For more details and a complete guide to canine acupressure, I suggest reading "Acu-Dog: A Complete Guide to Canine Acupressure" by Amy Snow and Nancy Zidonis.

Chapter 5: The Importance of Brushing: Understanding the Canine Skin and Coat

With a good understanding of how the canine skin and coat is supposed to work and how we are supposed to properly condition them, the finished haircut almost always takes care of itself. We should first know about the anatomy of the canine skin and coat and how to properly prepare it for a bath if we are to groom our dogs properly. It is like painting a wall properly. If all the proper steps were taken, the new paint lasts a lifetime and never bubbles or chips. There is much to learn and always more information being discovered about the amazing dog, and we often take the fact that they are amazing for granted, only seeing them as little furry humans. We often make the mistake of assuming that their skin and hair work the same as ours. Dogs have much thinner skin than our own and their coats are more of an extension of their skin, which is why it grows all over their bodies in order to provide them with protection from the elements. I will cover some basics about the skin and coat so that you will have a basic understanding about how the dog's skin and hair are designed to function. Hopefully it will spark an interest inside of you and you will continue your research into the canine skin and coat. It is a fascinating topic!

The first thing we should cover is the cellular makeup of the canine skin. Dogs have five epidermal layers of skin cells that are the same cells but in different stages of life. The dying cells are at the top layer and these provide the first layer of defense. Each layer beneath it are skin cells that are healthier and provide other vital functions, but they are "decaying" and are constantly being pushed upward toward the top layer where they will finally die and flake off. Skin sheds just like their hair, but if the cycle is normal we usually never notice it. When we wash our dogs, we are stripping off the skin cells at the top layer along with the natural oils. The skin will react by going into overdrive, producing more skin cells faster to try to replace the ones that were "attacked" at the surface. This is why we can eventually end up with a flakey, greasy dog. Why would a dog have flakes and greasy skin? It is confusing because the flakiness would indicate dry skin, but the oily coat would indicate an overly greasy skin. It is because when washed improperly, meaning without taking the proper steps, the skin continues to overproduce skin cells and oils to replace what it thinks is constantly being stripped off the surface. It is all happening on a cellular level, which is why it takes so many years for these symptoms to start becoming problematic. We can never escape the accumulative effects of years of repeated cellular damage. A good groom always stands the test of time.

When a dog is groomed the skin cells reproduce faster, thus resulting in a thicker skin that flakes and is more prone to skin issues. This is because when we wash and clip the dog, on a cellular level what we are doing is attacking the skin. The skin reacts by going into overdrive to try to rapidly replace the skin cells that are under attack on the surface. In my experience the effects are usually excessive dander and dry, flakey skin. This condition is irritable for the dog so they tend to scratch and chew at the areas that are the most irritated, and this causes sores and raw, bald patches on the skin. However, every dog is different and some dog's skin will react by becoming overly greasy and oily. It looks like they have hair gel or oil in their coats at all times. This happens because the oil glands have kicked into overdrive as well to replace the oils that are being washed off the surface of the skin. These oils also carry a scent which is why the dogs tend to smell stronger and more frequently when washed too often. All of this is working on a cellular level so we never even see the damaging effects until it demands our attention. We never even see it coming, and most people attribute it to the dog's age. The effects that we can see show up several months and even years down the road. It is an accumulative effect of years and years of attacking the skin and coat due to a lack of information – not bad intentions or a lack of love. That is one thing to always be careful of is that good intentions are always good, but if the impact that our actions have on others is a negative one than we must reevaluate our actions. We must pair our good intentions with the right knowledge on how to properly condition, style and maintain a dog's skin and coat.

In my personal experience most adult dogs that get a short puppy cut, or summer cut, on a regular basis have skin issues: bumps, lumps, skin tags, fatty masses inside the skin and tumors, hot spots, etc. The way to stop all of this from happening is to share this information with other dog owners. "Brush more, bathe less" is what we preach at our salon to our clients. We educate each owner on the skin and coat and how to properly maintain their dog's coat. If more people realized what they were doing I believe that the vast majority will change. The "Summer Cut," a very short cut that even double-coated breeds like Huskies have been known to receive during the summer months, should actually only be done during the fall or winter when the sun is not so intense. Huskies will actually stay cooler during the hot summer days than a short-coated Pitt Bull can because the thick double coat acts as their naturally air conditioner. However, during the fall and winter they can get too cold if they have no coat to protect them. So actually, it is never a good time to have a "Summer Cut" done on a dog. These are, of course, my own convictions based on my own experiences and research. I am not condemning anyone who makes a living doing summer shave downs or judging anyone who prefers short trims. I am only sharing information, and encouraging a shift in the way we look at dog grooming. In the end, we must all do what we know in our own hearts to be right.

The ideal situation would be to brush out the coat daily to evenly distribute the natural oils throughout the coat. This keeps the skin and coat healthy and you will notice a brilliant shine to your dog's coat. The colors will pop out at you, and your dog will carry himself with more pride. By brushing you are also pulling out dead hair that has lost its color, and along with the hair comes the dander, dirt and cellular debris, and cellular buildup that was all inside those pores. You can actually see the little specks of cellular debris and dander on the base of the hairs that are on your brush. Just imagine that was all inside of the skin. So by brushing daily you will actually see a brighter, shinier dog that smells less and sheds less. They actually look nicer the less you wash them, which is hard for us to understand because our skin and hair works differently. I must shower daily or my wife will not have me next to her in bed. The differences between our skin is just a small part of how different we are and how differently we experience the world around us. But dogs are the only animals that can connect with us so naturally on a spiritual and emotional level. To me there is nothing like the connection I feel with a dog.

It's hard for us to imagine because with us it's one hair per follicle, but with dogs every follicle is jam-packed with hair (up to 25 hair strands) and cellular buildup (oils, bacteria, dirt and debris, etc). By properly brushing we are helping the skin breathe by pulling out dead hairs that are in the pores waiting for new hairs to push them out. Any dull hair you see on the top layer of the coat, you should be able to just pinch off your dog effortlessly and a chunk of hair will be in between your fingers. Now look at the base of the hairs and you will see small dust-like dander that was pulled out of the skin along with the hairs. You have just helped clear out that pore – you've successfully carded the coat in that one area, and it was much easier than you thought! By doing this we are giving the dog comfort and providing healthy conditions for the skin to flourish. I love how happy the family is to experience how wonderful their dog can look and feel, and I'm sure the dog feels mighty proud of himself too! To me there is no greater service to others than to help them feel happiness and joy.

The difference between a proper groom and an improper groom is usually not obvious the day they are done. However, just like a paint job, an improper groom cannot stand the test of time. If the walls were not prepped or the painter cut corners, the paint will bubble up or chip and eventually peel off. It may take few months or a few years but you can never cheat the test of time. A proper groom has lasting effects that continue to enhance the dog's natural beauty. They will grow out evenly and smooth, looking nice for several weeks after the groom. The rewards of a job well done continue to last long after the job is done. It is like carving out a beautiful statue. It doesn't matter how hard or which way the wind blows. Even after the storm has passed, the statue will stand.

Understanding the skin and coat helps us understand the importance of brushing before the bath so that the shampoo will be able to best condition the skin. "Humanity before Vanity" is the motto in the grooming industry. Brushing the coat out before the bath is important, but what if the brush will not budge due to a matted coat? What if the dog is matted and tangled up all over, but the owner does not want the dog shaved? Is it possible to demat a matted dog? Yes, it is possible. I know from first-hand experience that dematting almost any matted coat is possible, but the question is how long are you willing to spend and is it humane to do so? In my experience, when a dog is tangled up all over it is better to shave the matted hair off the body and start over. It is very hard on the dog to endure a long dematting session no matter how good the products and tools are, and some dogs are just not willing to tolerate it. However, everyone has different circumstances and different dogs – you must be the judge of how much dematting you should do before deciding it would be best to shave.

Whatever you decide to do, always make sure you are keeping the dog's best interest in mind. This will win you the respect of the dog. My personal opinion is that it is better to shave if it is a solid mass all over the body – pelted to the skin. I will try to save as much of the coat as I possibly can if there are just a lot of pin mats and tangled dead undercoat. Everyone has to make the call himself or herself, but I think we can all agree that if the dog is not able to tolerate a dematting/detangling session it is in the dog's best interest to just shave and start over. The dematting process can be long and laborious for the groomer but even more for the dog because we are constantly pulling at their skin. Either way it is always a good idea to wet the coat before starting anything. I like to use a tablespoon of conditioner in a spray bottle mixed with water. Spray the entire coat until it is thoroughly wet all over. This will prevent breaking live hairs and will help the tangles slip free easier. Remember, this is a labor of love and it will require your time, effort, and patience.

In regards to how often you should brush your dog the text book answer would be daily. A dog's body produces an average of 60-70 feet of hair a day according to Muller & Kirk's Small Animal Dermatology. But my daughter's pediatrician told my wife and I something during our last visit that helped me understand how to explain this much better. He told us that it is better to brush our daughter's teeth once a day but to do it thoroughly rather than 3 times a day and miss spots. I thought that was a perfect way to explain to owners how often we should brush our dogs. It is better to brush once a week but do a thorough job rather than daily and only brush the topcoat. It is difficult to find the time to brush them out every day, especially breeds like Siberian Huskies or Portuguese Water Dogs. However, if we can find time once a week to spend brushing and carding out their coat thoroughly, the benefits are a beautiful dog with less health issues – particularly regarding skin and coat health. We also have a dog that deeply appreciates you for taking care of all her needs. Grooming is about trusting each other, respecting each other, and loving each other. I'm amazed every day at how much they are willing to give us in return for our time and affection. I believe that our time and attention is the greatest gift we can give to another.

Once the dog is all brushed out, and the areas that are to be clipped short are all clipped they are ready for the bath. This is the perfect time to go on another walk with them as a reward for their cooperation and patience. Clear your mind during the walk and enjoy your time together, and feel good about yourself for helping your dog's skin by clearing out her pores. I understand this takes time, but to a dog LOVE is spelled T-I-M-E. Now visualize a beautiful bath time together where you will further help her by conditioning her skin and coat. You do all these things for her because you love her and she cannot do these things for herself. You are love in action. Everything goes exactly how you want it to because Love is the most powerful force in the universe and you are wielding it the way an artist wields a brush. This is the Art of Grooming.

Chapter 6: Bathing and Drying: Working with Mother Nature

One day my dog, Dexter, decided to groom himself. I was horrified at what happened. He found the nastiest patch of grass, possibly a dead animal, and rubbed his neck and chest in it before making doggie-snow angels on top of it. When he came prancing back to us so proud of himself, we all screamed and made sure he stayed off of us. When I finally got him to not smell so offensive after several rinses, he looked so disappointed and upset at me. Baths are unnatural to dogs; we often have to stop them from rubbing themselves on the ground after the bath because they are trying to re-scent themselves. They groom themselves by rolling around in grass or rubbing against trees, but in order to live together with us in our homes they must not stink. The smell usually comes from the ears, feet or the sanitary areas. Before we actually wash them, we must first clean their ears and sanitary areas.

Ear plucking is a hot topic among groomers. Some say to pluck the ears – pull excessive hair out of the ear canals – others say not to. From my own research on the subject, and my personal experience working with hundreds of dogs over the course of my career, my opinion is that if the dog's ears are full of hair we should pluck them out if there is no sign of an infection. Most dogs do not have hair that grows to the point of blocking airflow inside their ears, but certain breeds do – usually longhaired breeds. When the hair blocks air from flowing through, the ear canal gets warm and moist inside. A veterinarian that I used to work for when I started grooming told me that a wet, moist ear canal that is full of hair is a breeding ground for bacteria and ear infections. The only time we should not pluck is if the ear is red, swollen or looks infected. If we pluck an ear that is possibly infected, we open up that fresh skin to the bacteria and/or infection. Whether we pluck or not, we should always give the ear a good cleaning with an ear cleaner that is made specifically for dogs. Always use cotton balls rather than Q-Tips and be gentle as the skin is very sensitive and can become irritated.

First we should discuss water temperature. Cool water is best for their skin, but if it is wintertime and cold out, lukewarm water is acceptable. Because their skin is so sensitive it is best not to use water that is too cold or warm because of the reaction it may cause the skin and the dog to have. I usually test the water on my inner forearm to make sure the temperature and pressure feel right. Using too much pressure can be harmful to their skin because it is like attacking their skin with bombs, and it may strip too many skin cells off of the top layer of the skin. It may take a while longer to recover from such an intense attack. If we are to attack their skin let it be more like swimming in rough waters rather than a tornado or hurricane sweeping through and stripping the oils and skin cells off of the surface of the skin. We recommend not using a jet stream or a high-pressure spray nozzle. I like to use a shower type spray setting with about the amount of pressure I would like when washing my own hair in the shower. Test the water pressure on your inner forearm, and if the water is making a deep indentation on your skin than you may need to lower the pressure. Remember, it is not the water that washes away the dirty hair and tangles. All of that should have been worked out prior to the bath. The water is to assist the shampoo and to rinse the dog clean.

Washing a dog is one of the most intimate moments of the groom. It is the part many people dread, but it is actually the part we should look forward to the most. This is the perfect time to incorporate our knowledge of touch therapy techniques. We now understand how powerful a touch can be when the intention of love is behind it. We are in a place of love and the dog will recognize it. They are sensitive to our energy and will understand us when we touch them with gentle massaging motions in order to bring their bodies to a balanced state. We are balancing their Chi by massaging pressure points in order to promote inner peace, healing and well being, and to strengthen our connection to each other. The moment I begin to massage a dog's head they immediately understand what my intentions are and who I am by the energy I am projecting. I could talk their ears off listing reasons why they should trust me and it wouldn't mean a thing to them. This is one of the greatest rewards in grooming is to gain a dog's trust because he is too noble and has too much integrity to sell out. They cannot be sweet-talked or conned – there is no way you will be able to bribe a dog that does not trust you. A dog's trust is to be earned by being genuine and by providing calm-assertive leadership.

I believe that I have come up with a way to incorporate the concepts of TCM with the bath. I call it an Acupressure Massage Bath. I believe it will give our dogs the ultimate bathing experience that will soothe, relax, and refresh the spirit of both the dog and the groomer. It is important not to scrub or use too much pressure. We do not want to irritate the skin or over-stimulate it by rubbing the surface too much while it is wet. The way to massage the dog effectively during the bath is to use your hands and fingertips like another dog's mouth and gently squeeze and release. It is more of a bouncing action rather than a sweeping or scrubbing motion. Most shampoos will require at least 5-10 minutes before rinsing. We must give the shampoo the proper time to work because it is ultimately the product doing the cleaning and not our hands. During this time is when I believe it would be perfect to give the dog a nice acupressure massage. The difference between acupressure and a massage is that we are applying gentle pressure to the pressure point sites rather than continuous circular motions.

Starting at the head and both ears, we will work our way down the shoulders to the center of the chest, down the front legs and paws, then down the back and work the body, and finish at the tail, hind legs and paws. This will help the process flow smoothly and naturally in order to help the dog feel comfortable with the bath and fully relax. This will also ensure that the flow of the water will help train the hair to lay naturally in the direction it should grow: "Always work with Mother Nature" my mentor, Cesar Milan, would say. Remember to visualize positive results, and breathe through your belly not your chest. We can take full advantage of the lathering process by using the dog's shampoo as a "massage oil" to help us work each acupressure point effectively. After the dog is fully lathered and you've massaged his whole body, follow the same path as you rinse the dog off to provide a "hydrotherapy" massage in the same direction the acupressure massage was given. A good rule of thumb is to rinse for at least twice as long as it took you to lather the dog to make sure he is completely rinsed out. Any shampoo left on the skin or coat will have negative effects.

It is not the actual rubbing or fingers massaging that are doing any healing, because if that were true a robot's arm should produce the same results as a human's touch. It is your thoughts and your energy that is emitting off of your fingertips. Without the loving intention behind the touch the massage would be meaningless. Have you ever woken up from sleeping because someone was sitting next to you? Or felt someone behind you before you actually turn around to see who it is? Try closing your eyes and have someone put their finger in front of your forehead and you will feel the energy that I am talking about. Most people usually do not need further convincing on this subject because there is something inside of us that tells us it's true. We all know.

When using shampoo, I always use the gentlest shampoo that is suitable for the situation. It is important to read the labels and the manufacturer's directions on how to use the product. I always read the ingredients to make sure the product is not loaded with too many chemicals. The fewer ingredients I see the more likely I am to try the product. It is also important to know what each ingredient does and how the skin will react to it; and with smart phones now we have all the information we need literally at our fingertips. Everyone is a genius now and we may as well take advantage of the technology available to us. Dilution ratios are one major thing that many groomers tend to ignore. Many shampoos that are available in gallon sizes or larger are concentrated and have a dilution ratio printed on the label – usually 16-1 or 32-1 and sometimes we have to adjust the dilution ratio depending on what condition the skin and coat is in. These companies pay scientists a lot of money to come up with these dilution ratios in order to provide the best results. When we use the shampoo at stronger concentration level than suggested or even at full strength, we are causing tremendous damage to the dog's skin and we will never be able to see how his skin is reacting to the chemical attack on a cellular level.

Brushing a dog's teeth is optional as there are many alternative ways to promote canine oral health, but if you choose to do so, now is a good time while they are in the tub. Always use toothpaste that is specifically made for dogs. Dog toothpaste is enzymatic, meaning the enzymes do the cleaning rather than the brushing and scrubbing action. Brushing a dog's teeth can actually be harmful to their gums. Use the toothbrush more as an applicator and simply apply the toothpaste onto the teeth. I like to use beef or poultry flavors so they think it's a treat and most of the dogs I see gobble it up. They were probably thinking, "I knew there was a treat involved!" Try to get some of the toothpaste on their tongues if they don't fight it because this is where a lot of the bad breath is coming from. This also gives you a chance to get a good look at their teeth to see if there are any issues that you may want to show the vet. Catching issues early is critical in addressing an issue before it becomes a major problem. In their natural setting dogs would chew bones and crunch them up to get to the marrow inside. This would clean their teeth naturally and keep them strong. We can mimic nature while eliminating the risk of choking on a piece of bone by giving them safe chew toys and dental treats. By keeping their teeth and gums healthy you can eliminate many other health issues. Everything is connected and one thing always affects another.

Once the dog is completely rinsed off it is time to dry them. Remember to rinse at least twice as long as you lathered. I usually encourage them to shake before drying them though because they do such a good job getting the bulk of the water off. One study found that dogs could shake off up to 70% of the water on them with a single full-body shake. I don't move out of the way when they shake because I believe that my body language is more important to a dog than my spoken language. I can tell him that water is ok and having water sprayed on him is fine, but if I move out of the way or act like I don't like the water being splashed on me than he will probably be led to think that I'm full of crap. Sometimes I stick my face in it to show them how much I love it, but that's crazy so I'm not going to suggest you do that. Sometimes certain dogs will not shake the water off even when encouraged to do so and that's ok. You never want to force an issue or feel upset in any way. Whether they shake or not it is a good idea to run your hands over them like a squeegee and wipe the excess water off before using a towel to dry them. This will prevent using more than one towel to dry them or using a damp towel to dry their back half.

A properly bathed and dried dog is such a beautiful sight! The coat seems to float and feels like baby rabbit hair. To achieve this beautifully fluffy look we must hand-dry, meaning gently brushing the coat while blow-drying with warm or cool air. Many places still use heated cage dryers to help dry more dogs faster without taking up too much of anybody's time. I understand the need for efficiency. I used to be more critical of groomers who run their shops like assembly lines rather than a salon environment until I opened up my own grooming salon. Now I understand the need for efficiency and profitability, which I will cover in another book: The Business of Grooming. However, the drying process is where most injuries and fatalities happen. Dogs cannot sweat the way we do and are much more sensitive to hot temperatures. They overheat easily and can have a stroke, especially if they do not have much coat to protect them. A full-coated Siberian Husky will be less likely to have a heat stroke in the summer than a Pitt-bull simply because they have more coat to help them cope with the elements. One famous case I read about in California happened while the dog was in the drying cage and the owner stated seeing bloody claw marks inside the metal cage. We can speed up other things about the groom, but we cannot take shortcuts to a proper drying – especially older dogs. We must work with Mother Nature, and nature requires our time.

Chapter 7: The Importance of Grooming Tools: The Groomer's Chisel

A comfortable pair of shears for a dog groomer is like a comfortable pair of shoes for an athlete. It tremendously helps our game. Practicing controlled movements and feeling comfortable cutting hair with the shears and clippers will help get over any nervousness you may feel about cutting dog hair. The tools should feel like an extension of your own hand. The best advice I can give someone is to go somewhere where you can actually hold and test out the shears before buying them. I borrowed money from my mother to buy my first set of shears online only to find out that they don't really fit my hand comfortably, and they are too big and heavy compared to the kind of shears I prefer to use. In Atlanta we have the Atlanta Pet Fair each spring and we usually wait to buy our equipment there at the trade show so that we can feel and test out the tools before buying them. I would highly recommend going to a grooming trade show in your area to actually hold and try out shears or any other grooming tool before you buy them. The people there will also have a wealth of knowledge to share with you as well like how to hold the shears for maximum control and proper maintenance.

Art is all about control. Beautiful paintings, beautiful music, and beautiful performances are all about control. The better you learn to control your shears, the better you can express the image you have in your mind.

The most important thing is to first see the finished look you desire and then snip off the hairs that stick out. Good grooming is not about how much hair you are able to cut off, but knowing where and how much to cut. A professional groomer doing a demonstration on a Doodle told us in the audience to "groom with structure and you can never go wrong." If you know the correct angles for the canine body you will know where and how to make each snip.

Using clippers is a great way to save time and set an even length when you're grooming a dog with long hair like a Golden-Doodle. A good friend of mine, and an amazing groomer himself, once told me that holding a pair of clippers should feel like holding a pen or pencil. It is a groomer's paintbrush. I have developed a slightly different perspective on the clippers. I believe it is the groomer's chisel. Michelangelo said of his legendary statue of King David that he did not create King David. He said he was already there and all he did was chisel away the excess. I believe that is what we do with our clippers and scissors. It doesn't matter what brand of clippers you prefer to use, they are just tools to help you chisel away the excess of a shaggy Lhasa mix to bring out the beautiful girl that was in there all along. Our hearts and your minds are the most important grooming "tools" we have, and our grooming tools are there only to help us express the beauty that is inside of our minds. Learning to use all the different tools and equipment is very important as a professional groomer and the knowledge of how and when to use them will be invaluable to you. Knowledge and wisdom come with experience, and there is no substitute for experience. We must do something over and over again in order to get good at it. Les Brown says, "Practice makes improvements, not perfect. There is no such thing as perfect. Practice makes improvements." Practice control because art and beauty is about control. Groomers must not only practice the physical control of our bodies and the tools we use, but control over our mental faculties as well. We must control our emotions, our thoughts and our feelings.

Our minds are incredibly beautiful. I know this because I see evidence of this fact all around me every day. I see pictures in grooming magazines that are breathtaking. Poodles that look like marble statues rather than live dogs, and Bichon Frise's that look like perfectly round snowballs. Those amazing haircuts first had to originate in somebody's mind before they became a physical reality. When I'm scissoring in the angulations for a Poodle I constantly remind myself that it is not my fingers or hands or my physical body that is designing the cut. It is my mind that is doing the designing and my mind tells my elbows to stay tucked in, my hands to hold the shears still and my fingers to make a controlled cut. It all starts with the mind, so clear your mind and make sure you have a clear image in your head of what you are trying to accomplish. Remember to stay focused; many unnecessary accidents happen because of a moment of distraction. I would also suggest looking at a lot of pictures of dogs that are well groomed. Perhaps Google search images of Champions to see what they look like and study them in detail. Once you know what the dog is supposed to look like, all that is left for you to do is to chisel away the excess. Be a Jedi Groomer using your shears like a Light Saber and your clippers is your Laser-Beam gun. If you're not into Sci-Fi, than you can pretend that you are Michelangelo the great artist. Either way put your mind and body in a calm, assertive state of being; visualize the finished cut and believe in your own unlimited potential. We can do anything because with God all things are possible!

If you are interested in proper breed patterns and learning how to set the lines properly, there are many great step-by-step guides such as Notes From the Grooming Table by Melissa Verplank. There are many other great breed guides available and many breed profiles and instructional videos are available online as well. These are all important to learn and to know, but what is most important is our approach and how we apply new information that is presented to us. My marketing strategy has always been how happy the dogs are to see me when they come back for another grooming appointment, and how calm and relaxed they are when they go home. If we take the proper steps before the bath, and take the time to bathe and dry them completely, the haircut and styling almost always takes care of itself. The groom will also last for months and grow out smooth and evenly. "The proof is in the pudding." Do an excellent job when carding the coat, and the haircut will grow out evenly because you are working with the true length after all the dead/dying hairs are pulled out. Most groomers I've met are perfectionists by nature – I've chased plenty of dogs around with shears because I saw a stray hair – but we can save ourselves a lot of time and headache by just properly carding out the coat prior to clipping and cutting.

Chapter 8: How to End the Groom

After the haircut is done I always shower them with praise and sincerely thank them for their trust and cooperation. Even if there were rough moments, we only focus on the good and reward her for completing the activity with us. I usually give them a gentle head and ear rub while feeling genuine gratitude and joy for this wonderful experience. Trust me, they will feel it too – it radiates through our skin and creates a field of love around us. Then let them down from the table by holding them close to my body and gently rest their paws on the ground. Do not let them jump down. Because we have just massaged their entire body, we must allow their bodies to set and relax in order to fully take advantage of our efforts. We do not want them doing anything too strenuous. Now is a good time for a leisure walk. What better way to end the session than with a walk: the dog's version of a nice chat. I noticed that every dog walks taller and prouder after a groom. They feel good and they know they look good – most can't stop prancing around, strutting their stuff. This is a victory walk where you both get to show off. This will ensure the dog will remember this as a pleasant experience and will most likely be willing to do it again. You should notice the groom becomes easier and easier each time you do it together.

Staying in a positive state of mind is crucial when the groom is over. Just like people tend to remember the beginning and end of a speech, dogs tend to remember how the groom began and how it ended. When the haircut doesn't turn out the way you wanted, or if you made a few mistakes, don't stress about it. Do not worry so much with how the haircut looks once it is done because this can ruin the experience for the dog. When we look at them with disappointment we are sharing negative energy. They do not rationalize the way we do and will think you are disappointed with them – they feel the bad vibes. This could turn grooming into a negative experience; one anticipated with anxiety. Once it is done, it's done. Stop looking at it, and remind yourself that it will grow back. Tell Buddy that the dip in his poofy head makes him look so cool and brings out his fun personality! He'll be in heaven, wagging his tail in ecstasy – he doesn't really care how he looks as long as you're happy with him.

Dogs will love to be groomed as long as we create a positive experience for them. If using a kennel to hold Buddy in, check to be sure it is clean and comfortable with fresh water to drink. If you allow the dogs to just hang out, have him rest in an area that is quiet and comfortable with easy access to fresh water. After a grooming session, especially if we are incorporating massage techniques, dogs need plenty of rest and fresh water. Strenuous exercise or excessive stimulation is not recommended. A leisurely walk is great, but not a jog. I like to play mediation or quiet classical music to promote rest and relaxation. Nothing warms the heart more than seeing a peaceful, clean dog cuddled up in his favorite bed fast asleep after a groom. That feeling inside is even better when you know that you are the one who created this beautiful experience with your own hands. You can do it – you have greatness inside of you! You are everything to the dog you are grooming – you're their whole world. To do this for them is to demonstrate and express your love for them and your gratitude for their loving devotion to you. There may be doubts and fears, but love awakens in us the courage necessary to act in spite of our doubts and fears.

I truly hope this book connects with you, and helps you if you have an interest in dog grooming. This book is my philosophy on dog grooming, and this is my art – my passion. I write this book to help dogs and their owners by creating awareness on the subject of proper dog grooming and the significant role it plays on the life of our dogs. My hope is that all dogs receive the proper grooming care they need by sharing the right information. Most skin nightmares that appear on older dogs are caused not by owners and groomers who do not care, but rather people who do not have the right information. By brushing and combing more regularly and washing less frequently we can save them from all the harsh skin issues that seem to be plaguing our dogs. It is not only causing our dogs to experience such an uncomfortable life in their later years, but it also causes owners so much heartache while costing them a lot of time and money at the vet's office. It is not a lack of love, but a lack of the right information.

In review, always concentrate on your breathing and how you are feeling first and foremost. Then visualize positive results and see yourself not only doing it, but knocking it out of the park! Believe in yourself! Be aware of your energy and use the power of touch to communicate your intentions. Be aware of each moment and read the body language of the dog. Be conscious of your own body language as well and remember to listen to your body. Readjust your stance and always find a comfortable posture while working. When I remind myself to breathe I am almost always suddenly aware that certain muscles in my body were tensed while I was holding my breath. Relax, breathe, and let your body be the physical expression of your mind. "Physically we don't stand a chance with unruly dogs. They are physically much stronger than us, but mentally we are much stronger than them" Cesar Milan. I believe that many of us groomers, including myself, suffer from self-doubt and our own insecurities at times. But that is only because we forget who we really are. We are artists – we are creators! We are fearless and courageous when we are called to be in order to lighten the burden of another. We do all that others may fear to do, or may be unwilling to do, because we love dogs unconditionally. Love is the most powerful force in existence. We are love in action, what is there that could possibly stop us? Our minds are an amazing gift from God. Once we realize and unlock our true potential, I believe that anything is possible.

Made in the USA
Columbia, SC
29 July 2019